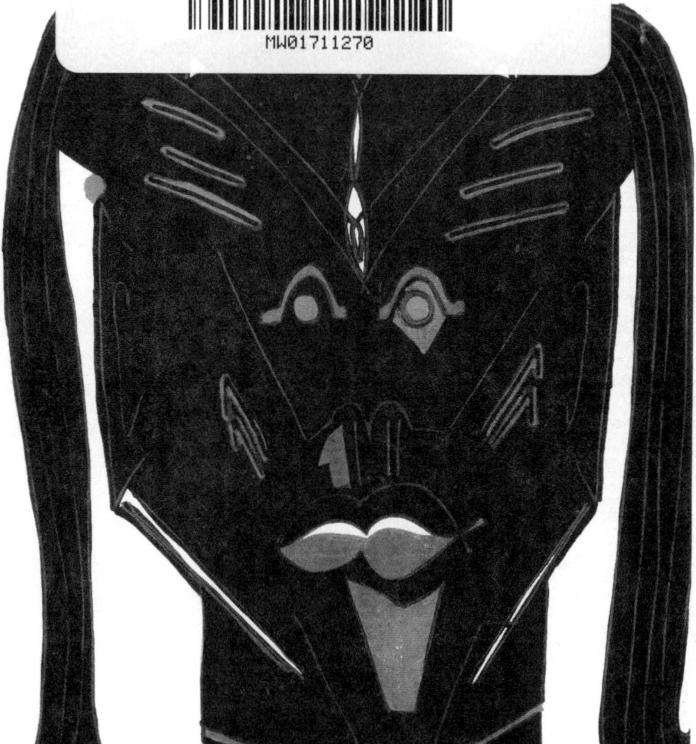

ELECTRIC CHURCH

ELECTRIC CHURCH

by

K. Curtis Lyle

introduction by

Will Alexander

BEYOND BAROQUE BOOKS — Los Angeles

First Edition

Beyond Baroque Books is an imprint of
Beyond Baroque Foundation,
681 Venice Boulevard, Venice CA 90291,
Tel. (310) 822-3006.

ISBN 1-892184-12-5

This is Volume 25 # 2 of Beyond Baroque Foundation
Publications.

Printed in the United States of America
by FineArts Printing Services 866.480.0550

This book was published with the assistance of the Lawrence
Lipton Trust, the Los Angeles City Department of Cultural
Affairs, and others.

Special thanks to Kayren Lyle, Kimberly Lau, and Will Alexander.

CONTENTS

Introduction

RE-EMERGENCE FROM THE CATACOMBS BY WILL ALEXANDER

When a true poet factors into visibility it is cause for excitement. It is to witness a new condensation of energy, with all its rapture and uniqueness. Not that K. Curtis Lyle has never appeared in print, or given readings, or read his poems in performance with musicians. He has nonetheless hovered in that zone of interjacence, maintaining a profile of fugitive incandescence. There have been poems printed in Quincy Troupe's anthologies *Confrontation* and *Giant Talk*, as well as *Black Digest* and other less chronicled journals, but appearance in print has been rare over the past two decades. His two books, *Drunk On God* and *15 Predestination Weather Reports,* date from the mid-to-late 1970's, and there have been no new books, and nothing I can note concerning individual poems anthologized during this time period. In this regard Lyle has remained a puzzling temperature, especially while writing with prolific concentration over the past decade and a half. Lyle works by the principle that if excellent work is produced, people will find it. This book is living proof of that principle.

His poems partake of both the telluric and the stellar—images erupt in the form of interior code, rhythms are aboriginal, powers partake of ferocious lingual audacity. A philosophical threading blended with subversive humour. In particular, I'm thinking of "Sometimes I Go To Camarillo & Sit In The Lounge," and "The Guerrilla Ecstatics." But if one looks through his whole oeuvre, the poems blaze, and concentrate like heat from concealed "scorpions." This is an organic Surrealism where a fish reverses its nature by loving "land" and fearing "water." It is not the subconscious welter of Surrealism as theory, but the ability to blink and see images. It is the Surrealism not of Breton, but of Tutuola, without having to move the stubborn weight of conscious mass. Lyle's images seem to naturally form into great non-linear lists. For instance, when he speaks in one breath of Emiliano Zapata, Bud Powell, Charlie Parker, and Diego Rivera, in the poem "Tampa Red's Contemporary Blues," or the catalogue of hallucinogens in the "Guerrilla Ecstatics." But the poem which struck me the most in this regard was "Poem In Quest Of The Pure Image." Everything was there: the "poisonous stone," the "electricity" of "eels," the "impregnable avocados." It is a poem tireless in its energies with its "mad-orange sun," its "remarkable birds," its "decibel of hyenas." The words explode and fly, and hurl themselves to the earth, while maintaining themselves in a state of simultaneous rotation. Reading the poem made me ecstatic. I realized that it was possible to conduct oneself this way in English. True, I had been in close contact with poems of Bob Kaufman and Philip Lamantia; I had read *The Palm-Wine Drunkard.* But Lyle was someone who had developed in the community in which I lived, in which I was questing for an ecstatic kind of language. I too had the fire of the seeker.

When we finally began conversing I felt doubly blessed, having the privilege of reading his work and conversing with the source. The conversations would take place in his house on odd Thursday or Saturday afternoons, discussing Kaufman, Paz, Cesaire, Rabearivello. It was grasping through dialogue the great legacy that informed us. Yet there existed this difference: I occupied a teeming proto-field, but it was Lyle who published his works in the realm of Hernton, Cesaire, and Neruda.

By sustaining our conversation over time, language and its reality as imminence began to magnify. I began to absorb this reality, giving me the confidence to take language beyond the pragmatic, the didactic, the plain spoken. These talks were organic for me; they helped sustain my first roots, growing as they were against the imaginal limitation expected of the Afro-American poet. I had yet to meet Lamantia and Kaufman, so Lyle was the first contact I had with an international rhythmus. He was composing a poem almost daily, which to this day remains an extraordinary sustainment. Witnessing such praxis gave me a double revelation; one: to hone each word, each line by means of the imaginal through intense aural condensation; two: to weave and develop these lines into anomalous interiorised epics. It was during these osmotic exchanges that "Asia & Haiti," and all the longer compositions I've subsequently penned were originally seeded.

Lyle's poems continue to free us "from the immediate images of perception," allowing us the realization to "absent" ourselves, to "make a leap toward a new life." And this "leap" was manifested by a concomitant social condition in the mid 1970's. At this time both Lyle and myself were members of an extended community which was not unlike the great Surrealist gatherings some sixty years earlier, or the utopian communes evinced by Fourier a century prior to Breton. One of our central hubs was the Broadway and Manchester local where the Los Angeles musicians Ray and Ernest Straughter operated a collective incense business. In essence it was an Afro-Surrealist hive frequented by poets, musicians, and fellow travelers. Rasul Sidik, Azar Lawrence, Kamau Daáood were spontaneous participants. There were others too numerous to mention. But it burned outside the stratagems of the academy, outside the fact of the rational principle. It peopled a zone that Parker Tyler has called "elsewhere."

This period has gone unnoted because it remains infortuitous with the media. It is not the Los Angeles of Rodney King, of the Crips and the Bloods, of the Black community as a conclave of crime and drugs. It was and remains a symbol for making great imaginal leaps. It carried on the great Los Angeles tradition of Eric Dolphy, of Charles Mingus, of Ornette Coleman, of Jayne Cortez, of the Watts Writers Workshop, of which Lyle was a founding member. It is the tradition of making magical art through experiment by lightning. Playing with parsecs of salt on the page. More succinctly put, the poetic plane.

And this is where Lyle has remained, on the poetic plane, linguistically prismatic, having passed through both the visible and invisible obstruction poets are wont to endure. You have here poems that have passed through the chrysalis of obstacle, without stuttering, without the crutches of academic encoding, evincing a luminous electrical scent, a music where the rhythm of passion is spoken.

ELECTRIC
CHURCH

TAMPA RED'S CONTEMPORARY BLUES

we are stranded here against a dark blue and shaded night
peering into these intelligent rooms
through the forested eye
of thirteen great atlantic owls
conjuring while conceived in the original blue bottleneck
of Tampa Red

black-inked leaves teardrop and fall toward
the unbearable street or sit dumbfounded
in corners
of chimerical ceilings
where we place our three eyes
under the melting pot
of ludicrous passion
and await that rude performance called the initiation
of the world, the opening of blistered and boiling water,
the translucent floodgates of incorrigible time
engaged in a dialectic
of wheatstraw and steel
or riding the australian crawling logs down market street,
speed boats contending
in the black plum trees, huge and scuffling
feet tangled in the buckling and bladed blood
of steaming and involuted roots
the initiation of the world, dark hands molding charcoal
into the artifice
of bleeding stars, the mouths intent
and drawn-out
against the still life impression
of our own navels

where innumerable fish owls seek the obscure identity
of woman

the initiation of the world, absolute and libertine fisherman
dying
        of freedom, their ox heads sighted beneath carnivals
of peasant women, rancorous and fucked-up mules thrown
into a fulcrum
                of wild nuts
and beaten under this composition
                                into a primeval cross
of woodcut carbon

the initiation of the world, perspiring and yellow moons
amid a sad procession of trees, through the sad night
an innocent man's blood caught in the sun
against the crucifixion
                        of evil and sad women, in the sad night
an alchemist composing cold and erotic ducks, under a sad tree
of the night we are waiting for a report
from Charlie Parker
waiting tables in Spain, 1939
or Diego Rivera, upside down scratching his ass
while beginning the construction of the new and
profoundly imaginary world, between shadows and mountains,
between drunken women and hod carriers, between some silver
altar piece and the portrait of a miserable stable
hoarding the angelic and allegorical eyeballs
of the heroic Zapata
we are waiting for Bud Powell
and the corn stalk
                    of nude prisoners

fleeing his persecuted and percussive piano
we are waiting for horses and their vestige, the child-figure
who will come out

                                        of his solitary egg dancing
and bringing us an essay concerning the moon
we are huddled and waiting, western and cowboy drunk
between the one colour of our malleable landscape
to see if this poem just rides off into the sunset
or really succumbs to a frightening and logical end

POEM IN QUEST OF THE PURE IMAGE

1.

an unbroken saturation of seven blueberries,
thirteen rainstorms of telepathic snot,
announce the architect of the moon's dead flesh
the sun's lucidity poured into breakers
                                        of impregnable avocados
as the sun's flesh turns a logistical yellow
in the black egg of the night
this is the language of space;
acute vowels sucked
                    through
a bowel of volcanic straw
the bowels of black mariners turned
                                        into
a pounding musician
and stretched like hide accents
over an expanse of mono-thematic cherries
lemon-lime sown into the glucose evening
at the word's insistence
at the moment of the word's death
its tireless life poured forth
                              again
from an instance of eels
from the dark mouths of electricity
poured forth
            from the mouths of poisonous stone
and incorrigible headache
poured forth
            from a black tympani

beaten senseless in cold snow
now an engineer of the stone's flesh
comes crying tearlessly
                from encountering wetness
he comes screaming from the ducts
                of an eyeless little girl
who
plucking fruit in the incendiary orchards
                of night
rattles her ecstatic fingernails
and cuddles celestial mosses
                in the cabbage rows
of a purple sun
a sightless little girl
who
breeds the blood of concubines
                with the soft lava
of nectarines
whose heads are sledgehammers
pounding plum trees
                into a crucifixion of marvelous
elephants,
the wings of remarkable birds
beating the gums and sucking the nostrils
                of infinite tornados

2.

procurers of dry blood,
vision of ruminating pimps pinned carelessly
                between seventy-three bronze
el dorados

3.

onyx born in the venom of bulbous snakes,
raised on the urine of mutant antelope,
and guillotined on the sky-blue altars
                                        of obesity

4.

O blood-red moon
come into my eye
on the electric intelligence of maroon rectums,
come into my eyes
                        on the gratuitous pubic hair
of tempestuous mulattos, come into my eye
on the supple tales
                        of tabasco-ed flesh

5.

O mad-orange sun
pass the decibel of hyenas, wed harlots to groundhogs
in the last centigrade
                          of the afternoon, urinate goat's milk,
cover your insatiable nipples with the dung

of a blue rhinoceros
and destroy the song in a transcendent scream
of cobalt melons

SOMETIMES I GO TO CAMARILLO & SIT IN THE LOUNGE

Sometimes I stare into an awning of spirit
and the prose of her son
burns my eye into a vacuum
of frozen blisters
Sometimes my face hanging its tongue
half-way between mechanized jawbones
and ancient skullcaps
Sometimes I-am-viewing the world as
yellow trumpets of starving blues
against a piece of body that used
to hold some Vietnamese mother's breast
or the ultra-high-frequency screams
of some stupid marine with his cold
fingers stumbling down past waistbands
and ending the milk of the life of some
heroic woman
Sometimes the nature of my sickness
a driving sunflower rain of stone
and seeds onto centipedes
the choral of my brutality
pulling fifty legs from a body
maiming it for life
Sometimes deep in the animated suspension
of my alconarcotic dreams
I am wishing for an act of holiness
and cleansing
I-am-wishing for an hour of napalm
on ALL Junior Chambers-of-Commerce

Sometimes
I go to Camarillo and sit in the lounge
fascinated
        by
incurable tics   on vacant schizoid cheeks
        I
sit and watch   spastic foam in the trenches
                              of madmen's mouths
the emptiness   of alienated sound   somehow
                              passionately colloquial like
                              truncated elegance   or   reams
        of   poetic potential rolling across
        asylum   floors for the dead heart
        of   emasculates
they (the inmates)   propped in gutters of cafeteria
their (funky)   bowels running thru America's
                              kitchen ascending minds transcending
                              the walls of room 305
they (the inmates)   a love conversation of sweet mangoes
                              to a nation of malarial armies
they (the inmates)   a continuous poem of bird-caged heads
                              battering-rammed against the
                              immobile word of corporate prophets
Sometimes   I-am-reading short stories
                              of Nelson Algren
                                      or
                              Pietro Di dinato
                                      and
                              ignoring whole epochs
                                      of
                              my history
my limbs   painting the grey factories
                                      of

the world   reds   blues   purple-blacks
—crazy colors for the fleshy segment
        of
my memory bank
my life   l o n g i n g l o n g i n g
for the women of Dahomey . . . and . . .
their strong thighs . . . blacker . . .
than anthracite warmer than fresh
French bread
Sometimes   late morning's motioning birds
pressing tired headlines of bitter skies
into my forehead
        puritas
water flowing beneath a burning bridge
        of
snowflakes
        and the
nobility of my dead grandfathers' ashes

deeper

deeper still
        till
lost in the interior
        of
God himself
himself   an irrepressible soul blowing
nuclear heroes
        into the
rivers of time
        and
space

THE 33RD DEGREE OF VIBRATION 218

I am the janitor of the soul
The bottomless double snake
doin a double take
at the dweller on the threshold of infinity's abyss
The upside down Caduceus throwin a spiritual hand grenade
filled with infra-red piss
The empty eyed block trio
the black chamber chimney sweep
the night howler peepin Tom's war lover
The fear merchant starch collar
tryin to sell myself like holy communion
The pain-soaked lug-head ultra-violet vamped-on
gas pig 22nd Solar angel of the bottomless pit
The 33rd degree of vibration 218

In concern I see your fear
In calamity I see catastrophe and stretched treachery
I look for love leakin onto hatred
I leach it and block its hat then pass it on to you
I have seen the mad healers of the future
dissolved by Neptune in the ninth house

I am the janitor of the soul
The cow-dung paper-thin bullshit window-washer
from the American winter of the west
The circular tantric mantra of deepening darkness
The molten root mandala of predestination weather reports
I talk shit and mean it

The craving of Olympia Jones for dry bones

The screech-howling pandemonium of the dung microbes
created in the valley of McDonald's who refuse to come out
The 17 billion pacifist warriors poisoned
are my most profound piece of work

Cleaning-up the world is the only job
of the janitor of the soul

MORTUARY SCIENCE

Desert man Thunder woman Shower child
Rain boy High Wind girl
Gale of the mountain frozen over fire
I do not predict the weather
I forecast the radio waves bent through the prism
of mirror stars
I suggest force
I answer the infinite need of coal to be diamond
I describe the solar chariot
I foresake the power of the center to show you the image
of the whole

River flow gram of soil balanced by the weight of fire
Nitro-ellipse the musk and the wave of the dead
challenge you to change and be nourished
by their immanent mortuary science

Phosphorous storm
Hail Stone stampede
Monsoon shaping the leaves of the world into pellets of tears
The chanting of stems
The roots of the depths charged with providing food
for the God of the depths

Masonic flower
Mason seed of the northern plains
Man is the mortar cementing heaven and earth
Man is the redeemer ark
Man is the revealer being
Man is the depth law of faith and communion

Man is the forge of erotic depth
Man is the 3 Aquarian dreamers
Man is the vault of the dead holding the invisible mind
stopped at vibration 235

MORTUARY SCIENCE MANDALA

We are rising from the sea
We are embracing dolphins
We are bent and augmented to the form of desire
We are impulse-pulse potentially planets

Spirit at work in the electronic sunset
Atone-tone-tune-tolls invisibly

A festival of flower tremor of joy tremolo

The cycles of collective communions
The startling substance of light in the consecrated city
reaching up to the whole wide existence of human awareness

Bridge across a deep motion gage
The legacy of the man-made canyon chasm grave opening
to release the link process of substance up
across the capa-city
These are the days of collective skill and conquest

Five-fold the features of the mind separate and identify
the devotion of harvest and work to the divine with pleasure
The sacred technicians flood the form with energy
and rebuild the body of stark intuition

The float flower of lotus laughing on top of the lake
delivers the sermon of the service root mud bottom song
The petalled balconies driving the gondola of the integral

If I cut you I must realize that I will bleed

Spirit is not a star
sequence is not a symbol
mental is not the mind
blood and water flow directly and actively into the love-call-real

Incandescent carnival

Interchange and commingling first
then inspiration from the depth of strength
from the seed of concentrated inner need
from the harvest of the thing sown
from the creation of clone from the seventy series
comes the engine rising in the back of the mind of man

Blessed is the song bestowed
Blessed is the spirit filled full
Blessed is field sustained the work done
Blessed is the soul released into twice one beatitude

The broken sleep achieved memory entwined to value
The struggle is founded upon its finish

Courage must be muffled against the cold
Character must be thrown against the universal crises and molded
Man must dare to charge the storm
Attack lightning crush silk the straw hat of ambition burned
at the entrance to the new level

Illumination is a canyon a narrow path an arrow seeking
the heart of a stone deep root elder brother dry bone
wilted marrow drove zen junctions 96 to 105 walk on

Love is the one
Love is the beginning
Love is the bearer of light and motion
Cupped heart far from the furnace of value
Explode the erotic God of the depths
Let the dream ride the real!

The sufferer sits alone isolated from himself
in air-conditioned darkness the guards drop candy bars
every three hours for his personal illumination
on thursdays the chaplin brings him the blood
of another recent dead friend and pours it in his eyes
This is for him the mystic company of perfected beings
This is for him the ordeal of liberation exalted

The last stage has now become the first
The slaves are masters of themselves
The intuitions are new the flesh fresh the theory
of organic rebirth now fact the tensions broken
The children of the tender virgins filled with tenderness

Revelation psychic sunboat structure the sea is wonderful
but I am unconscious and cannot breathe
I need the open window the glass-bottomed wine of my reality
The underside inside the depths of my mind
is now translucent
If I can swim and breathe at the same time
I'll be all right and eagerly real
The flag turned into an eagle
The eagle turned into the eye of a man
Searching for his shadow
his eye went out

and he then became the ear
of the planetary rhythm
It told him to look ahead and plan

Mountain stream
clear up the day like you did the night
I want to be the star in my nature
I want to be poppy source not drug or transference
but source I want to be poppy source
I want to be mountain rock celestial canyon pure alpha
delta soil seeking the level of water
chill morning dharma imbibed
I want to be seven dreams flowing irresistably

I want to be eagle dream
The straw on the floor of the stable of the new age
I am bold enough to ask for a little help
the power to rise with purpose
the power to fly high the power to live in the focus of the sun
the power to be one of your heralds the power to crow
with the crowning chanticleer the power to drink resin
and resonate
the coming of new days
If you'll just announce me I'll be there

I want to be eagle dream streaming consciousness
Mud floor dog day looking only up
Pierce my shadow the seance of the meadow calmed by rain
The disappeared pain turned to ecstacy and Saturn joy claim
the future of the planet and I'll stake it out for you
The tender care of dawn cradled
If you're able to announce me I'll be there

UNEXPECTED ELEVATION

Communion Tao-Taos the eagerness of the blue lake
to expand the balance inside the anvil
of the conscious crack of seed-spirit
rhythmics the sole initiation
God I am your channel your fifth avenue feeling dispossessed
and dissolved and deliberately opened
to your spirit-source healing service
to supply what I need
Collect me here in the channel of motion and force
without interference
If the nature of my next joy is accidental
I will cherish it
If my fortune lies broken and fragrant in the dust
at the close of my 43rd sequence I will still surrender
my mind to the public realm of your mass intoxications
The power of your psyche pierces space beyond the shadow
of biology because power here is the personal ritual
of communion pounded by the sea
The dark-root deep-sea diver gold rush laser-shattered value
unexpected elevation bathed in green moonlight
calm quiet opening of skulls to a higher inspiration
God I want to report the weather
and if you let me report the weather
the ark of tears and rain and human scalps unleashed
the earthquake surge that follows solitude
the penetrating power of a tantric mind absolved of separations
the center of the elemental cross exalted
will overwhelm the things that were illumined
and unseal the things themselves perfected and illumined
and unlettered

NIETZSCHE SAYS LIVE DANGEROUSLY. WHY? BECAUSE IN DANGER YOU ARE THROWN BACK TO THE *HARA*. YOU CANNOT THINK; YOU CANNOT WORK THINGS OUT WITH YOUR MIND. YOU HAVE TO ACT IMMEDIATELY

The Book of the Secrets, Bhagwan Shree Rajneesh

Blessed is the Black Neptune Warrior passing through
the center of the one-water bucket found
passing through the magic grasp of the primal soul
the feeling-fire arrived at the chord of celestial depth
the core of the somber fable whole
Blessed are the ovum temples
the satyr-root-rope dancers debating shadows
Blessed are the plantain omens of the diamond south
Blessed are the pestilential peacock consummations
of shattered cobblers and adepts
Blessed are the three dreamers of the burning revelation
Blessed is the war-wagon the chain-link camel slope the mortar
of the sunboat
Blessed are the men who are woman-seeker-warriors
Blessed is the woman who researches the direction of man
the visionary redirecting the pole star of value
Blessed is the bio-spiritual-spherical maidenhead innocence
and its mother-memory and its father-fear delivered
from wintered darkness and rigid ritual
Blessed are the empty grape stains partner-creature buds
dancing in the final crises
of a young girl eating birds in winter
Blessed is the rainbow genesis the clover-faith communion
the love-death ceremony the spinal-widow searching

for the end of things
Blessed are the open graves the decaves of Sadhuhood
and Buddhahood
Blessed is the slave-bell chamber glowing in the root
of consecration
Blessed is the storm-chant-growth oceanic spiral
of virgin space
Blessed are the people singing laser-song into the end of frost
Blessed are the landowners conjured-up out of
one creative imagination
Blessed is the water of truth
the horse arrow sabled to the book of open straits
the all-love witness the rabid genius the love functionary
of the heaven-funnel
Blessed is the danger void the hara herald
the invisible double head of Hacho-Rah

THE KANSAS CITY TAO OF PHYSICS—FOR MONSOON WISDOM AND CONQUEST

Stumbling is divine work
The selflessness I once saw in nature
I now see in you
The Daud consecration I see in your chart
may push me to my limit
may pierce me through my karmic dung deposits politically
may redeem the unconscious collective sediment
witness that is my due

Planetary stumbling is divine work
and believe me mama the stamp of stumble seal
the seal of stumble is also the judgment stamp of you
Because when I am stumbling you are stumbling too

Remember now that Stumbling is divine work
from the cycle of fulfillment filled full of defeat
to the pen-poem of the complete surrender of the self
I would sacrifice my self for you
my spirit-freedom my uncontrol the three modes of my nature
the master of my head my super-mind divine workings
my devotion motive my mental heart flesh the mystery
of my eagle boy my tri-pathetic dark exalted emotional calcium
my lower liberation tongue my daring gnosis dew
my action-soul my penetration instrument
my higher visionary song
my Choctaw gong of action-time the subjugated ladder
of my spine
I would sacrifice myself selflessly for you
because I know you would do it for me too

But the Kansas City Tao right now moves so very slow
That I'm afraid your faith might break and run from me
thinking that what it sees is one more tragic ego
one more lower gnosis seeking fraud attainment
one more self-perfected fool chewing
on the shadow of illusion
one more double-tantric mildewed heart farting into space
one more vial of elemental vocal tricks
one more bull trying to fulfill his raja-biosphere
at your expense

Stumbling is divine work
because I am not of this life
I am not this stream of light
neither am I mind or body or life or thought
or whirling doer dissolution void miracle center
dynamo birth abstraction dream

I am only the bumbling stumbler divine working
of points and fields and magnets
the yielding of the law of invisiblity Godhead
swallow session extracting exaltations
And like you I am grains of cosmo-sand beached
by God and water-logged
I am only divine stumbling milkweed metaphors
I am only the end of everything searching for beginnings
I am only the deeper descent of wildness not the deepest just
deeper than the rest
I am only the rabid millenium seeking rapidness
seeking penetration seeking mind-turns and pure-force
seeking not to kill a fly seeking not to harm a soul
seeking the old dark conquest possibility of breaking
all the things that came before

I know I can't go home again
But to just stop and say goodbye to that
the thing that made my gut leak
made my mind kiss discontent
and chocolate chaos on the mouth
To say a deep goodbye to that makes my other heart long
for death
or dread or Jah-locked toxin bread or anything that will
fuck me up for good

Stumbling is divine work
and I long ago consented to the charcoal song of dark divine
and you consented too
to be dark and bitter-sweet
to have your meatless ass trembling
to have your real life begin as the starkest drama
of your life
To meet me somewhere near the Kansas City Tao of physical
free-mind roamed through floating intuition
depth communion
cherry-bombed equinox
We are being born
We are being born into desire-fire
We are being ridden hard into fall
into the ultimate tests of fear and its ferocious ovum teste
confidant pain absolved of absolution
We are being burned in dark ablutions
We are making love in India we just think we're in the west
That's what the Tao will do if you follow it too far

Stumbling is divine work

THE EXHAUSTION OF THE MIND ATTEMPTING TO PENETRATE THE MYSTERY OF GOD

Mind will destroy everything. Marriage means mind. Love is spontaneous; marriage is calculating. Getting married is a mathematical thing. Then you wait for those moments, but they will never come again.

The Book of the Secrets, Bhagwan Shree Rajneesh

This tale is happening to everyone
The processional motion of life
is happening to everyone
The constant changing of one thing into another
is happening to everyone
The chemical biological nutritional terrestrial solar
galactic ablution is happening to everyone
The spirit in the star of healing
is happening to everyone
The temporary sperm-drought Plutonian victory of woman
is happening to everyone
The exhaustion of the mind of man attempting to penetrate
the mystery of God
is happening to everyone
The million diverse bacterial mushroom layers of space
are haunting everyone
The Oyabe x-ray spasm of cloud rickets
are falling on everyone
The solution to the mystery of iron breath turned
to copper bile
is waiting in the deep kidney-liver-spleen-heart-lung core
of everyone

Doyo O Doyo O Doyo of hot-fire of wind-wood of cold-water
of dry-metal of the steel-sweet-retarded earth harmony
lives inside of everyone
The organ of bitter-blood complexion
The sour Neftali muscle nailed to black-blood island
sparrow-sperm
The hairy salt of bones and sympathy consumed by grief
The lid-lipped sweet flesh maroon song taste of death
The smell of nostrils withered skin the things we loved
but left behind
is alive in everything
Doyo O Doyo O Doyo

GOD IN THE DEPTHS

Doyo enraged between eyebrows
Doyo leaf-cogwheeled blossom
Doyo belated lotus loa-Neptune carnation
Doyo interior eye and eye
Doyo healing of color and light
Doyo the tone of the nation crawled under a rock
Doyo this is why the chanticleer praises the milk
of the maggot
Doyo the knowledge of human desire
enraged between eyebrows
Doyo planet tongues enraged between eyebrows
Doyo black amber bear clan clarity fog
in the valley of bewilderment
Doyo interior eye and eye enraged between eyebrows
Doyo aloe unknowable musk enraged between eyebrows
Doyo the volcanic volcano burst in the colon
Doyo the eruptions of condors and hawks and
the semen of eagles
enraged between eyebrows
Doyo the flower-seed the muscle-lung-loin-membrane
the bellows of breath the rivers of blood expelled
to make room for the wine-wizards the drouth-froth charts
of eternal progression the Sun-elevation of judgment
and conscience the proto-soul of love and death
enraged between eyebrows
Doyo the red phallic dog empties his bowels on the throne
Doyo the Eskimos chant the elevation of winds
Doyo the gas-cloud-sun-molecule merged with the Sun-vapor
that was soon to be known
Doyo the duckshovel quacked under the weight of its madness
Doyo the bamboo armature cracked under the weight

of the dawn
Doyo the elegy of asphalt was the only song of the soul
Doyo the pulse of the empty heart-gong in repose
waiting for impulse
Doyo the yellow jaundiced foot sacrificed at 1 and 11
enraged between eyebrows the purple rishi collecting
the zen quarrel petitions of unbending intent
Doyo the elevated song of personal garbage
the gong of elemental trash ringing through the world
Doyo elevated contempt cracking the bosom of night
Doyo blooming the crimson of bloodclot paroles
enraged between eyebrows
Doyo the dao of the tao walking calmly between Xiron and Zion
Doyo the shoulder of the horse ridden
becomes the house of the leper
Doyo the nipple of day is harder than the nipple of night
Doyo I have penetrated the city of the future
and I have kissed the charcoal God on the mouth
Doyo I have vomited-up the elemental law
of boiling chrysanthymums
Doyo she-the-shaker-of-my-nude-depth
is descending into dawn into doyo-compost
into rage into doyo-the-depth-of-gangrene
Doyo the unknowable root of primal life
Doyo the path through the core of my wife
is the nectar road is the bliss trip compounded
by thought and then overcome by the death of the mind
Doyo stops the world doyo does not do doyo kicks back
Doyo drinks itself consumes clone after clone
ravages zeros ravages zeros ravages zeros
enraged between eyebrows
Doyo has penetrated the city of the future
and kissed the charcoal God of light on the mouth

TUMOR IN THE WOMB

We ate the bark-flesh dinners beyond distance
We ate the eucalyptus cuisine of the fresh water forest
We swallowed the pellets of reindeer
trying to remember the waste of their horns cold astral magic
We inhaled the autumn-dead-sun secretion of bees
from Korea
because we thought they would untangle our blood
We rescued subterranean snails from banana slug deaths
only to find them bitter in the bile of our livers
We swallowed the path of the sage
and he burned down our need to consume
We found the tumor in our womb and fed it
back to black termites
We swallowed 68 Hokkaido plums in reverence to salt
We inhaled the werewolf sperm of the white-jaguar-bat
balm in the licorice kidney
We caught the cold light of august bleeding
The silver chute of meteor rhythms
We made the Afrikan barysphere vomit-up gold
We made flower-death subside
We made the power-pulse-music crank-up
the unitary primal engine
We followed the 2 with the octave of 2
We entered the tomb of the triple shield with the talisman
of black perpetual federation
We reported the weather according to the old rules
of the bound mytho-gangsters poets zircon freaks moon dust
stargazers
We invented cyst-solitude and then destroyed it with tumorous
chemical mat spray out of boredom

BIRD RITUAL: LIGHT IN AUGUST

Ritual Bird
Liturgical Star
Pearled Chalice Bearing Ash
Axe Woman Dusk Sustained
Mother of the cloven hoof kamikaze music
You who brought the alto saxophone
of the last black wanderer
west
and made him equal to the light of August

Ritual Bird
Liturgical Star
Pearled Chalice Bearing Ash
Axe Woman Dusk Sustained
Mother of the cloven hoof kamikaze music
You who bent your alto breath inside the bright mouth
of the last black wanderer
and then turned the motherfuckah
into a blazing light in August

Ritual threadbare
Ritual birdsteer
Ritual toneflow
Ritual mountain
Ritual silence
Ritual number
Ritual bearclaw
Ritual waterfall
Ritual sunwolf
Ritual separation

Ritual integral
sky cap dry skull
chamber of the corpses piled high
dragon's head ritual daughter of the fruit fly
in
tegral float
fire boat of the trigger happy harlem loas
in
tegral float
fire boat of the trigger happy harlem loas
in
tegral float
fire boat of the trigger happy harlem loas
unleavened sanctified bread and water
unleavened sanctified bread and water
unleavened sanctified bread and water
the answer to the material question
is the answer to the quota of the world

Ritual somber
Tropical stride
Integral wrestler of death
The hip bone is the high water mark of the abyss

What heals you in heaven
may poison you in hell

Ceta of the rump sitar
Bottle neck of the blue pork butt
Five reeds hold the thunder breath
of the raggedy black bird
and five ass planets heal his turd devotion

I believe that this is the beginning
of something entirely new
that has been done many times before

Ritual stark life
Ritual dog stare
Diatonic drama of my lips saga bull sage
roaming the world by freighter
Ritual seashore
Black sand ritual of marginal clot depth
Clinging deep zone absolved by the sweat of zeros
can these be the songs of psalm chaos?
can we be the soul's merchant seamen bearing fish brains?
can there be anything cool restored to the cold deck
scurvy and misery and lame duck catastrophe?
where are the heroes of texture?
where is the wet squad that brings quiet drink and warm food
to the shores of the sundrought world?

Ritual navel
Resident cord swallowed by nitrogen thought
Ritual kidney waxed to the ear of the world
Who was the last bell to overpower a flute?
Who was the last woodblock to fall beneath crocodile tears?

Ritual river run over cliffs
into basins and bottoms
of timber stained tributary river beds
Ritual stone ground down to flake and to shale

Ritual bird broken like houses exploding form
come through the hole in my chest to the NOW

of the world to the time-core of moments
redeemed and restored
where you bent your alto clay breathing to bear
like lasers reborn
inside the soft fleshy mouth of the last black wanderer
turning and turning and turning into a light that makes light
more brilliant than beauty in August

RITUAL: DANCE AT THE END OF MY RAGE

I was a singer for sixteen years
I was the nude ice cap transmitter enraged
I was the reindeer reception for floe
I was the jelly roll meat shaker of shin bones
I was a singer for sixteen years

My hand was my blade and my chalice
holding my head late under the cold weeping of night
was my pitiful leisure
My celibate sensual coughs dropped sperm and mole lettuce
into the ducts of the women who carried my daughters and sons
I was a psychotic breast pump engaged to a militant razor
I was the weary milk of a bottle numbed and stamped
into glass

I was a singer of work songs for thirty-two years

Now the cell drummer at the end of my rage
Now a dance at the end of my rage
Now the stage-coach blackberry action-eater
dead and alive at the end of my rage
Now the illumined number multiplied
into the end of my rage
Now the bugler of ritual bombs dropped
into the end of my rage
Now a hawk saddle invented by loas
and ridden straight into the end of my rage
Now a speech mule hoof shaped like diamond sweat
dripping a bilesweet dread
dragging a known sucker a long song locked into itself

and dying slowly
Now my mouth tastes like something that could only
swallow itself and continue to think
about the shape of alone

I was a singer of work songs for thirty-two years

Now I am throwing my voice out of my throat
Now I am molding my heart into a tear
Now I am ripping the coleus scabs of the wind
Now I am the lead chamber of stark Zulu sex
Now I am the washerwoman of the spears
Now I am the emotional twisted tide of blood moons
Now I am the white Choctaw dog eating crows in crystal-fog
Now I am a butterfly satyr forming the dance
at the end of my rage
No longer a song
I am the dance at the end of my rage
The flesh-rock meditation
The cremation of fire in hands of the drummers
No longer a song
I kick the maypoles of the night and they grow strong
I grease lightning with fishes and pigs and they are intentions
grown stronger
and request that they too understand the center of strength
that dance is the rotating rage of fishes and pigs
of fishes and pigs of fishes and pigs of fishes and pigs
No longer a song
I am the eel mode of massed love
the gathering together of the throng
dancing
into the end of my rage

I would go straight ahead
but the ritual road is curving for miles
I will go straight ahead
no longer a song but only a dance Zimbabwe
Akka
Meroe's deep celebration turned into cash
and then liquid ash dense lymph busted seer
uprooted and then stomped beyond the foundations of breezes
into the last image of dance at the origin end
of my rage

SPIRITUAL: BILL

He asked the most high God
to square his flowing sun alone
beneath the sun banner of the double sage

He made us seven at the gate
Kamau the gentle fighter of the sun and moon
Ojenke the raging essence of love
Curtis just turned forty into the spirit of sunwolf
Yasmeen a black woman whom I do not yet know except
as a grape-bearing star
Shams the perfumer and the bearer of the perfect mantle
of the diehard
George Quant whom I have seen twice for the very first time
and Bill
who made us seven at the gate

He asked the most high God
to square his flowing sun alone
beneath the sun banner of the double sage

Bill you are alone
Bill you are alone
Bill you are alone
Bill you are alone
Bill you are alone
Bill you are alone
Bill you are alone

PROBE: EVERYTHING IS NOT ENOUGH

Mother of light am I stone
that I should be challenged by the water core
of cosmogenesis
that I should be stripped by time
that I should be beaten down this way
into one fine atomic powder
that I should be whole love stark and staring
 into essence and quintessence
 like an eerie cryptograph of silence
that I should be blown polar mad by the solar wind
through all known unknown directions
that omega bleeding serpents through the cataclysmic points
of cold anointment
should bring my taloned five star breath to death
Mother of wood am I the group bark blindness shell
of lame dog kindling
that fire should burn me up this way
that words should hold me to the surface
and never reach my depths
is my vanity so hard
is the mast head of my day to day emotion so slow
that calling down the massive vengeance of mass purity
is the only chance I have to reach the land of Sufi
Mother of metal am I lead dicks forged
Mother of stone am I bellow rock root sand
am I anything that even moves inside or outside of form
Mother of earth am I moron song turning imbeciles to coal
am I so despised that my initiation should be cobalt harsh
should be devil glow
should be hell hound trick dark unconscious notion quick

should be ocean blur uppercut should be gut ripped
blood sipped angel head shit tipped spirit
Mother of everything must I give up everything

LOVE IS THE LAW: FOR AMOS

"When I was born," said Ogotemmeli, in illustration of his argument, "an equine antelope was born too. The antelope's prohibited animal is the panther. A panther was born also. But the panther's forbidden animal is the antelope. The circle was thus closed and complete."

Marcel Griaule with Ogotemmeli
from *Conversations with Ogotemmeli*

1.

An ambush
is a trap
in which concealed persons
lie in wait to attack by surprise

Love is a law
that is to be used
wisely

2.

When we are born
as animals
an animal is born
with us
And in return for the animal's birth
the animal lives to protect us

But in return for this protection
we are bound by duty
and by the law of love
to protect
that animal

And that animal is bound
by the spirit
of the law of love
to intercede
in our behalf
when we are down
or beaten or broken
or driven underground
by our detachment
by our own stupid originality
by the celibate need to crumble
the guerrilla seed
of those we feel have double-crossed us
by the emphatic fountain
of transgression and silence
that we all both hate and adore
And that animal is bound
by the spirit
of the law of love
to intercede
in our behalf

3.

You had cupboards full
of herb

but I had no mushrooms
I had an astrological chart
but no known ID
you had an identification
a driver's license
a blood type
a passport and an IQ
I had a chromosome
a gene
an archteype
a tongue on fire
from disuse
and the absolute abuse
of trying to break my own
unknown record
for passionate and continuous
opposition to everything

I saw you as a hero
and a giant and a solo
Virtuoso
completely patterned
after your own finale

You had cupboard-full
of herb
but I had no mushrooms

4.

There was a white bull
in the room

when I was born

No discipline no self-control
No restraint no moderation no sacrifice
No patience no simplicity no humility
No knowledge no bank account

There was a white bull
in the room
when I was born
A snake and some oak trees
a goat and an ass
a dolphin and a foolish lack
of mind and word

5.

Mystics centaurs satyrs fairies
forests
meadows full of chinaberries
Exotic plants and natural food
drugs and wine
to change the mood

Wood and mud
and loam to paint
Thunderbolts
to crack the solitude of saints
Beauty savagely indulged
women used to soothe
the stupefying dirge
of Kansas City

Oily hair spilled on the floor
resource used to seek splendor

NO discipline no self-control
NO restraint no moderation
NO sacrifice no patience
NO simplicity no humility
NO knowledge
NO bank account

6.

The butterfly is
the white bull's
sacred cohort
His prohibition is
to do no combat
with butterflies

Strikin by the river
Struttin on the farm
Spiral in the country
Siren of the warm
deep cliff
that used to be the pasture
that used to be the well
of the future

A flutter shake
jerk
quiver quake
A sudden move past blinding speed

past blinding speed
past blinding speed
is the leitmotif
of the butterfly

His emancipation
His self-liberation
His openness
His free dome
brings home
to the white bull
the full impact
of the song of butterflies

Do no combat
with butterflies

7.

Pine oak cedar birch mahogany
humidity
the season of moisture
raining the body
in the sauna
of the full moon

I have been through many changes

I have always made love in the open

Planting my muscle

in the music of religion and medicine
I found a house
that longed to be a temple
A rose garden
of mysterious physicists
biologists
who refuse to leave the forms
of nature

8.

I will my mushrooms to you

CHOCTAW WEDDING

Blessed is the man who dies
            before he dies
Blessed is the woman who perishes
            on her wedding night

I took her to an altar
            of cornmeal
Where she broke me, unsealed me
                and made me tremble

Bruised, stoned and ruined
              like the sun locked-up
Like the heart of a lion
        reined in and pitted
        dug in and fitted
        against his will
        into the larger plan
        of Holy Zion

Blessed is the woman whose navel unravels
                  whose need
                  traces the people
                  back to a pumpkin seed

Blessed is the man who knows
                his own blood
                so well
                that he can tell other men
That it is the process of becoming a woman
                  that makes him wholly human

EVERYTHING IS WAKING UP!
EVERYTHING IS WAKING UP!
EVERYTHING IS WAKING UP!

The crow blows down the gap
                    in the wind
The mustard seed spots the corn
                    being born
                    and clings to the spirit
                    of becoming
The bluejay stands up and talks to the snake maiden
                    on the snake mountain

Blessed is the man who signs his name
                              in bone
                              whose signature sings
                              and inscribes spring
Blessed is the woman who shields the world
                              against the rage of the people
                              when they are frightened and alone
                              and being baked between
                              two hot stones
                              when their crooked mouths
                              are being straightened
                              in the smoke

Blessed is the woman who washes her face
                              in the presence of coyotes
                              who eats black meal
                              and assimilates one dark corn message
                              who blows it out
                              through the old hole in her belly

and then sends it back
to the soil

EVERTHING IS WAKING UP!
EVERTHING IS WAKING UP!
EVERTHING IS WAKING UP!

The man who met the red deer
is here!
he's here!
He walked all the way from Montana
using a red bandana
for his bedding
He came to see the Choctaw wedding
of the locust man
and the spider woman
of the antelope woman
and the eagle man
of the young humpbacked flute player
and the ancient soothsayer
of the hot ember
and the sandstone
of the icicle boy
and the horned toad
of the holy oil
and the milkweed
of the wild grain
and the bamboo reed
of the bean house
and the copper tooth
of sunrise
and the water moon
of big horn sheep

and blue earth
of the black seed girl
and the deep well
of the squash flower
and sagebrush
of hummingbird
and mountain lion
of medicine wheels
and sunshields
of midnight
and high noon
of cocoon
and universe
of precious salt
and pilgrim

EVERYTHING IS WAKING UP!
EVERYTHING IS WAKING UP!
EVERYTHING IS WAKING UP!

THE GUERRILLA ECSTATICS

It had taken them
nearly twelve hours
to disassemble the building
and another twelve
to pack it up
in the Volkswagen Van
which left them
the thirteen men
who had been recruited
for this special job
only 24 of the originally allotted
48 hours
to get out of the country

Like eagles
who had waited a lifetime
to find the serpent of their dreams
The Harlem Kleptomaniacs
gathered themselves for the one great flight
that would finally create their myth
and mark them once and for all
as the guerrilla ecstatics of the century
and lift them out of the category
of historical nuisance

T Bone Taliafero Walker
who had assassinated Pope John XXIII
late in November of 1992
with a specially developed
anti-clerical made-in Compton Marxist-Leninist
exploding cigar

broke out 14 grams
of pure fuck-Alberto-Fujimori-Peruvian-Shining-Path-flake
and laughed softly to himself
in that sweet southern morning maple syrup kind of way
that was really the only legacy that his daddy had left him
He reached down for the silver tablespoon
that certain homies had claimed
was the only instrument left on earth
that would fit his nostrils
because after years of snortin-up the best blow
on earth
his nostrils had flared out to such an extreme degree
that in every place he arrived
announced or unannounced
large crowds would immediately form
and begin the incessant and hypnotic chant
"Breather, Breather, please, save some air for us
please, Breather, you know we got to breathe"

As he began to break the flake down into powder
with the miniature Turkish scimitar
that his aintie Mabel had given him
for his twelfth birthday
he suddenly recalled an article
he had stumbled upon years before
in LOW DAYS
the international dope magazine
whose reputation had been built
on telling
who what why where
and of course when
in code
any kind of dope in the universe could be had

and for what price
The article had appeared right before a famous
black comedian-genius-storyteller-fool
had set his little narrow ass on fire
with a secondhand junior high school chemistry set
He had cooked up a combination of Hawaiian smoke,
Chilean-government-approved flake, Outer Mongolian
Rum, Lebanese hash oil, Chianti, French-government-
approved heroin, Mexican mushrooms, Congolese-my-
man-Mobutu-tested ganja, Jamaican lambsbread,
Dahomean Rada root
and New York State tap water
and then
he just blew himself up
(and they say we can't think in abstract terms)
Anyway LOW DAYS had implied in an editorial, a white
bread dope editorial, that niggers had turned cocaine
into a dangerous drug
just as the Jazz establishment (whatever that means)
had once tried to pin the demise
of every nickel and dime motherfucker
who had ever tried to locate narcotic heaven
without a functional compass
on Charlie Parker

Whatever

T Bone shivered
as his spirit approved the flake
then shattered the glass
that was once the windows of his soul

And then
he flew away

WORD FROM JOHANNESBURG

I receive the believer
Who was charred by the fire
I accuse and accept
The perennial liar
I take pleasure in setting
The day on top of the night
My historical measure
Becomes the wedding
Of the black and the white

The people decide
Not political whim
Human beings once blind
Look out over the rim
They see the weeping
Of blackness
They hear the confusion
Of Boers
They feel their knees once
Rubbed down to bone
Now redeemed at the shores
of counsel and home
That care could workup
Into the marrow and blood
That love could become
The herald
Where hatred once stood
Is a tribute to patience
And to faith and to man
Recognition

That courage is at the heart
Of the plan
It could all end tomorrow
or become the fact of the ground
You make the call
Tell me brother and sister
If what was lost
Is now found

Reconcile and then wed
No more guilt
No more sin
The jailed and their jailers
Close the wound
Heal the limb
Hatred is futile
Revenge is absurd
This is the word
From Johannesburg

THE SHAMAN JULIUS ARTHUR HEMPHILL DRUNK ON GOD

1.

I say God great and good God
I say master living clear in my mind
this morning
I say God great and good God
I say pearled dirge of scattering dusts
I say precious lord of old trails and places
nobody knows
I say unknown God,
sealed God,
fish God,
God of the hand stretched forth into the wound of the hip,
deep sea diving God the Father
from dark pools bending, wooded God,
Lord alone in the ninth remoteness of the forest,
distraught God doubling the velocity of the breezes
barking and splitting the sea
I say good morning God great and giving

2.

here
we string ourselves together in the prescence of God
we draw our fine bow
we break our bracelets above our brows
here
we catch the Lord mighty and uncaged, crowned
in St. James this morning

3.

we're gonna go to work this morning
warmed steam shovel,
mellow dump truck,
lumberjack of heaven who built the first lamasaries
in the firmament,
rejected angel calling down Jupiter and digging us
out of our minds
this may be the last time we read your letters this morning
but you can believe
we're gonna go to work this morning
our feelings and our muscles will be changed,
carried forward with flowers in our mouths this morning
and you can believe
we're gonna go to work this morning

4.

Oh blessed children
turn down the meter of my heart this morning
I say it pounds too hard for what I have to do this morning
Oh blessed children
I say Oh blessed children do you want to be like me
do you want to be like the old ones with feathers
who came up out of the sea
do you want to watch me
I say do you want to watch me disappear this morning
eased into a river of shale on this easter morning
the flow of my love's body burned up
like the incredible glow of a bird's dog
I went like a river of charred wood this morning
I chose my mama

I say I chose my mama
she didn't choose me this morning

5.

caterpillar boy bred on an idiotic future of sugarcane
this may be the last time we'll sing together this morning
the last time we cross the great streams
the last time we have wet dreams and are not ashamed
this may be the last time we uncoil the black eggs
that foretold our country
crane girl crying like a young earth cactus
crane girl, beautiful bird to be fond of you
is only joy, is only lust for the salt mother
reversed in charcoal, is only a passionate devotion
to the heavy womb, is a mile of pleasure from a little mouth,
is only love's delight in the spirit of the hidden world,
is only love's embrace where the world becomes huge
beyond all understanding, is only love falling disconnected
like a chanted song from the second stanza transformed, is only
love's feast in a famine of street corner marshes, is only
love's last meal exploding as a mountain acsending through
the point of a lake, is only love as a penetrated place
where the disappearing God said I would disappear
and it could be the last time
we make love this morning
crane girl,
corn snake sliding through a stem of tropical grass,
delta of disappearing powers who does not try to disappear
this may be the last time we pray together this morning
magical night,
purple heart ground down to nothing,

long white silky mane,
perfected path rolling through an agile chaparral
before daybreak,
eye of the morning meshed with the texture of quinine
and peachstone
this could be the last time
we kneel together in grace this morning
this may be the last time
we catch the lord mighty and uncaged, crowned
in St. James this morning
because the whiskey breath hounds of hell
are dancing on my trail this morning
lapping up my scent
talkin about the ground shattered and rent by my shadow
talkin about the ground might come apart this morning
but I'll be lookin good this morning
because I'll have disappeared
I won't be here this morning!
and it could be the last time you see me full
like the moon, soul like a spoon shakin off
this mortal body, gonna put on immortality,
gonna disappear in the middle of the air,
gonna meet my master God great God somewhere
this morning
and it could be the last time I get high this morning
and it could be the last time
that I break in the wind way up in the middle of the air
this morning
I feel linked and powered this morning
I feel strong
I feel solid and perpetual this morning
I feel like a dope fiend who's cleaned out his body

and watches its once soft resilience
fired like desert stoneware and rebuilt this morning
I feel hard in the heat of this morning
I feel cooled in the fold of the cloth this morning
I feel like a spinning and hanging man this morning
I feel like a medicine man who can heal himself this morning
I feel like the gong the gong that grows from power

6.

friends, God has mercy this morning
friends
I say friends can you hear God great God have mercy
this morning
I say God great and good God changed six miles to three
on my journey
this morning
I say God great God come down here this morning
I say God greet and good God
beat me for a drum where the water falls
like eight blue stones into clouds of smoking coral
like a leaf tumbling off a tree
shout me down and leave my thunder teeth drying in the sun
this morning
I say six white horses gonna come for me this morning
because Death is my mate disappearing and shaking my hand
this morning
this world is a whirl of acrid mountains this morning
but don't nothin bother me this morning
because I forgot I was a Man this morning
and the Lord let me weep this morning
and I'm so glad this morning

and if the Lord lets me sing this morning
I won't have to try and disappear
I'll just be gone!
and it could be the last time I get happy this morning

7.

Oh numb and distant lily of the valley
Oh unbearable sailboat of invisible skies
Let Me Bear You!
Oh vassal of the secret self
God great and good God
Oh black lattice strung and mounted to heaven
Oh Bright And Morning Star
this could be the last time
we shine together this morning

8.

Oh God great and disappearing God
if you are caught mighty and uncaged, crowned
in St. James this morning
then this is the last time
then this is the last time
I'll see this place
this morning

THE DOMBI

The authors of the Caryas saw the Dombi as the representative of "emptiness"—that is, of the unqualified and unformulable Grund, for only the "washerwoman" was free from every qualification and attribute, social, religious, ethical, etc.

Mircea Eliade, on India, in *Yoga: Immortality and Freedom*

The exemplary love remained that which bound Radha to Krishna—a secret, illegitimate, "anti-social" love, symbolizing the rupture that every genuine religious experience imposes.

Mircea Eliade, op. cit.

1.

Whore
Higher than the step ladders
that reach past giraffe pussy
I wait for you
in the perfect speech of scorpions
in the deep world of the mothers
and the motherfuckers
whence comes all beauty
and all beasts (it surely makes no difference to me)

I wait for you in the overwhelming births
of old children

At the central moment of eclipse
my eyes appear in the soles of my feet
searching for you

in the final collapse of Wall Street
I pick through the rubble of capitalism's
disintegrated genetic code
but always searching for you, for you!

Virgin
Dead
Homeless
Man or Woman
beautiful healer down on your luck
in the alchemical reality of the late twentieth century
through the power of love
I hunt you down like a long shot
I search for you by pressing my lips to computer terminals
I seek you out even in the solid state
where there is no more image of God
only the endless charge of human improvisation
I reach for you like a dark horse in the reversal of time
or as the miraculous woman
who taught me
that the blues is closer to nuclear physics
than meditation

I search for you where
serpent becomes redeemer where
poisonous fungus becomes sacred mushroom where
left-handed tantric master becomes dry saint where
great qabalist becomes wandering mendicant friar where

conch shell becomes black rainbow
I search for you in the long shot
the dark horse
the miracle

Through terror and wonder
Through disasters that renew life
I look for you in the globe of trees,
in the kiss of rocks,
in crystals and earth cells
in the most primitive salts
in exalted immobility

In ferment sediment fluid
From the utterly refined
through the unconditionally volatile
I search for you, for you, for you!

2.

I want your mouth
and your limbs
and your tongue
and your loins
in the dead droning night
of great jeopardy and great opportunity

I want you and don't know you
I need you and can't find you

Back through the maggot dawn of the west
I have chased you

I have chosen you!
I have chosen you!

I have seen you dancing in the tightness
of waterproof sperm and of frogs
I have decoded your voice in the livers
of dolphins
and still you don't come!

I have spread you out in cornflower gestures
and begged you to give me the sign
that doubles the spirit and makes matter
from shadows and songs

Like sixteen hundred years of radium diffused
in a day
I want you like the worm who loves sundogs
Like the fish that loves land and fears water
Like the eight shining peyote lizards
with nails in their eardrums
I need you like the right time to make rain

The enemy of God
and of nature and men
I wait for you,
four steps from light

BLACK CROW: THE MYSTIC MIGRATION OF BEN YORK

I took my time
Makin up my mind
About goin back west
I was a free man
In Tennessee
But It wadn't
the best life
For me

I had a mule train in Tennessee
But It wadn't
The best life
For me

The white boys dismantled me
In Tennessee
They took me
Apart
One day at a time

They did it real slow
So it didn't seem like a crime
But they did it just the same

They took us all apart
Like that
One name
One day
One city

One freight train
At a time
I didn't mind at first
I was thirsty for success
Had my freedom
And my free dome
I thought I was in a good place
What we call the 'zone'
So I quit payin attention
Til the day they stopped me
At the state line
And said mine was a strictly *intrastate*
run
I mean
How one man gonna make a success / how he ever gonna rate
If the best bidness is between Tennessee
And Georgia or Mississippi or Arkansas
And he can't leave the little yard
Of one state

I mean
If you gather up all your wheat
And all the alfalfa
Corn
Oats
Barley
You can bear
Where you gonna sell it
If you can't leave
Your little yard / if you can't get from here to there

I been thinking hard about this

About the farms
The stores
The stations
Where I used to sell
Hell
I was the best damn
Driver and seller
That any 'fella' ever did see
And now they can't kill me or sell me
So they gonna control me

They say I can't go to market
I can't advertise
Can't promote
Can't distribute

They say I got to sit
I got to settle
I got to wait
While they horde and monopolize
And speculate

I been thinking hard about this

When I was in the service of Captain Clark
Trekkin through the Indian nations
I got standing ovations
Everywhere I landed

I remember meetin a Black man
Who was a Crow chief
Had five wives

Fourteen children
Twenty horses
Six feet ten inches
From the crown of his noggin
To the tip of his big toe

I mean
What mo' do you need
In this life
But a woman and children
And a yard that big enough
For runnin space
Place was like that
Had an admiration about it
Nation full of warriors
And some good lookin women, too
I knew I was in the real world
When a young girl
Called Black Moon
Come over to me
And rubbed my arm
Like I was some kinda charm
Or somethin

Exact time
They understood exact time
Not clock time
But real time
It was affectionate and official
And always right
Their eyes were filled with light
But the big chief told me

That the people
He called his people ‘the people’
Were gonna disappear soon
Said it just like that
Without sadness or vexation
Said his nation was gonna disappear
Because sooner or later all nations disappear
Asked me to tell him my favorite dream
Before I went on my way
So I recalled the one that day
Where the rat sits on my shoulder
And gnaws my ear til my head disappears
I was fearful of that one
Because it would recollect itself
Three or four times a year
He laughed
And said I feared it caus
I didn’t understand it
Said the rat was eatin my head because my head
Was keepin my heart from talkin
To what he called the great spirit
He said don’t fear the rat
Let him do his job
Get rid of your head so your heart
Can talk
to the great spirit

You know
I walked
All the way back to Tennessee
Thinking about that talk
I had with the big chief

I been thinking real hard about this
I don't think I'm gonna miss Tennessee
And I sure aint gonna miss
What them white boys done
To me

I think I'm a' go
Back out west
Find Black Crow
Find the big chief
See if I can find myself

Captain Clark and Mr. Lewis
Were always good to me
They would talk a lot about
Ol' Tom Jefferson
And then read to me
But, you know,
I don't think they ever saw
My humanity

I think
I'm a' go back out west

I think that's the best place
For me

I'm a find the big chief

NAT LOVE: DEADWOOD DICK

Chilly is the rain
That remains of the winter
Enter now
The wind
Where sin brushes the ground
Like three-goose down
At the edge of the meager plain
That stains the cracked stone outskirts
Of Deadwood

Hollow are the thighs
Of saloon and whorehouse
Sunken are the eyes
That burn into you
Like pistol-whipped falcons
On a millenial mission
Of hatred and love

Above his waist there are doves
Of genetic history
There are European waistcoats
Cut with Cree and Shoshoni Choctaw and Cherokee design
The kind
That indicate the early
And beloved encounters
Between the strangers and The people
But
Below his waist
There are Pawnee medicines
The club, the bear pants, The bag of pochah bones,

The blade
That made the settlers wish
They had settled somewhere else
The ice-age arrow with the black head
That made the settlers' daughters
Shove themselves into the magnetic aura
Of Nat Love
Never realizing that he was Nat
Only
Above the waist
And that
Below the waist
Where their haste and greed and sexual needs
Had mistakenly directed them
He was Kongo hard
He was Mississippi mad
He was nigger slick
He was a cowboy on a mission
He was Deadwood Dick

RETURN OF THE DARK MESSIAH

"All those ships that never sailed
The ones with their seacocks open
That were scuttled in their stalls ...
Today I bring them back
Huge and Intransitory
And let them sail
Forever."
Bob Kaufman from *The Ancient Rain*

Pawnee Chief Patalasharo
Said: "I give you back your blankets
filled with smallpox, your guns and your knives.
I listen once again to the Buffalo; he tells me
these lives of suffering and disease are over,
finished, diminished, reduced to prophylactic
cinder; he comes through me with outstretched
arms and says, here, take my Buffalo body for
your food and clothing; he says, here, take my
bones as tools to cultivate the ground where
you grow your corn; take me home with you
and live forever."

Wovoka of the Paiutes dances
and his dance resurrects Sitting Bull and Big Foot
and the murdered mothers and babies and warriors
are lifted up by the intense love
of
his dance
His dance decrees the closing
of the long death trench

at Wounded Knee.
The mothers and the babies and the warriors
return
not like remembered corpses,
but as spiritual cordwood standing straight again
like the sacred trees
from which they were first made.
Wovoka of the Paiutes dances
and lifts up Sitting Bull and Big Foot
and the murdered mothers and babies and warriors
are resurrected and begin to live forever.

The steel mill in Gary, Indiana that killed Danny Serrat
The food stamps that humbled Charlie Richman
The fast food that altered the brain chemistry
of Cairo Clemons
and sent her mad and nine-millimetered into McDonald's
one dog day monday morning in November
as a hit woman
settling corporate scores
at the behest of Burger King
All these things are reversed
Danny gets paid for his labor now
and his labor corroborates his wealth
Charlie now has universal health insurance
that guarantees the removal of the food and drug stamp
from his forehead
And Cairo Clemons, who was once declared brain dead
now deciphers her food in a delta garden
coherently and deliberately
And Danny and Charlie and Cairo
begin to live forever

Uncle Ben and Uncle Joe
who missed the train headed north
because they were too poor to purchase tickets
are now awarded first class cabins
on the Lakeshore Limited, the Yankee Clipper,
the Southern Pacific Sea View, the Vancouver Express,
they have finally landed on the right track, they are
now attended by their progeny, as elders should always
be
they can now trek through plains, the swamps, the deserts
and forests are for their pleasure
as they begin to live forever

LEMON'S HOLY BLUES

three trees are standing on the ledge
            of my heart
three trees are standing on the purple hedge
            of my heart
three levels of unleavened bread
three pinches of crude sea salt
three unilateral pieces of flaming lard
all the wretched bones
            in my body
broken
all my veins burst
and three welcome trees are moving
            in discharge
across the ledge
holy
across the purple hedge
                        of my heart

LEMON'S WARM LIFE BLUES

draw a mole from its hole
          singing
burden my warm life, my wife
with a pigeon's egg
rolling me fast in chicken fat first
for a moon rock
                    and a dollar seventy cents
an hour

put me down
          under the ramparts
lay me out screaming
                    in a creole graveyard
howling jelly under thunder
                              in the hoo doo night

at sunset
          singing
draw a soul from its hole
sucked along the street
          bent
into a surah like sperm
its blue canal
               becomes natural history

LEMON'S AT THE SHORE OF THE WORL BLUES

first
the fierce medicines of eternity
rolled themselves into wild oats

then a forest steps
on his mother
and each tree
becomes a night howler
multiplied
by another sacred mathematician

NCE

oot
for m... fire eater

for fifty years
drink a kettle
of boiling water, fire eater

for fifty years
break out the wild heart
of a fast woman, fire eater

But after fifty years I got a new start!
come through the slaughterhouse,
fire eater
the woes the world
a simoon
of shambles

you have attained repose, fire eater
an absolute psalm
the lemon dance, you have intoned
a canticle of zeroes

you fire eater
your finger makes the simple
double curve against the flesh
of the fiddler crab
and a beak song
a bag pipe becomes a yellow mushroom

the first sound, fire eater

the protean act
becomes the air tight pit
of a purpled tiger plum

LEMON'S FIXIN-TO-DIE BLUES

I was fixin to die / get the cosmic boot
I was plannin to uproot my life
strip my bush & blow out its green
take the trees out of my mouth
clarify my flesh & tear out the place
where it became fluid
cast out my soul
break & immobilize my jawbone
lay down like one cord of steel
rusted & bound in clear water

I was fixin to die
five times howling
the charred meat of my water-frozen heart
like the earth cracked open

I was fixin to die
let myself fall away into a hundred pieces
bet each piece scorn the other
& let each part impale itself high
on a white-tipped wave

I was fixin to die
bit by bit
but I didn't

LEMON'S LAST-DITCH-HARMONIZE-MY-BLACK-MULE BLUES

harmonize my black mule baby
with a prayer
like a soothsayer
like a sweet potato
from the piney wood

harmonize my mind baby
with a heart in your left hand
hung low-down
like a finished woman comes
complete
like a free wheel
like the south-east wind
standin in the back door
wailin
a long musky peter-pushin poem
like the earth opened-up
like when you went into the black mountain
and dragged my rag doll home
harmonize me baby

harmonize my body baby
like your right hand weepin
like a crack in your face
mended
in catfish blood
my body baby
like a water trout
like a water saint
stompin a submarine

in the mud
my body baby
like a man learn to love you
ride you
when he calls your name
like when you starvin for a reason
you eatin just the same
like when you ragin
tumblin through the world
screamin
you still stakin out your claim
harmonize me baby

renew me baby
with a gambler from Louisiana
with a tramp from New Orleans

renew me baby
with a derelict from the bowery
with a nigga rebuilt in his beam
with a Lemon restitched in its seam
renew me baby

recreate me baby
on a saturday night
in a fist fight
that stops short of dyin
recreate me baby
like a ramblin man
with his nuts pulled out of the sand
finally takin off his clothes
recreate me baby
in darkest blue

in a deep pallet on your floor
recreate me baby
like sun bowels drinkin the ocean
like a blue black sperm
like a glow worm
shot straight through your twilight zone
recreate me baby
fill up my black mare
and let her run on out into the world
somewhere
and let her moan
cryin & sighin
recreate me baby

resurrect me baby
on King street in Dallas Texas
standin pat in my stetson hat
with a bird dog in a bag
resurrect me baby
on Prince street in Savannah Georgia
in a buggy
on a mule in a boogie
for a mile
with my feet wrapped in rags
resurrect me baby

rescue me baby
when I'm hungry without money
when I'm broke down an awful thin
rescue me baby
when I'm standin in the rain
spittin up sour dough biscuits
& suckin on a bottle a gin

rescue me baby

reclaim me baby
put harmony on my body
put humility in my mind
reclaim me baby
slow me down
strip me down and purify me
while I'm circlin the world
in stop time
reclaim me baby
take out my streaks of mean
put my second mind somewhere
it wont care bout bein seen
reclaim me baby

love me baby
love me

forget me baby
forget me

caus
you see
it aint hard to be a fool
when you been a black mule
long as me

harmonize me baby
harmonize me

LET'S TAKE A RIDE THROUGH THE COUNTRYSIDE:

We stop at Aketi, eleven times
We pass through Bandundi, where there are twelve gold mines
Beni
Boma
Bukavu
Bumba
Bunya
Butembo
Demba
Gemena
Dilolo
Gomo
Ilebo
Isiro
Place that God marked, ground zero
Kilemi
Kamena
Kananga
Kasongo
Kikwit
Kinshasha
The heart of the Kongo
The heart of the Kongo
Kisangani
Kisangani
Kisangani
where attitude rules
Kolwezi
Lubumbashi

Home of holy fools
John Coltrane
Luwebo
Manono
Matadi
Mbandaka
Mbanza Ngugu
Mbuyi mayi
Mwena Ditu
Panda Likasi
Port Kindu
Chikapa
Virunga
Watsa
Yangambi

JOHN COLTRANE!
JOHN COLTRANE!
JOHN COLTRANE!
JOHN COLTRANE!
JOHN COLTRANE!
JOHN COLTRANE!
He really loves Patrice Lumumba
He really loves Patrice Lumumba
He really loves Patrice Lumumba
JOHN COLTRANE!

The year is 1960
The passage is to darkness
The focus is diamonds
The target is the diamond mine at Luisa
The problem is the diamond mind of Patrice Lumumba
JOHN COLTRANE under the guide of divine love

Che sees the Kongo as a vast diamond in the rough
He sees Lumumba as not tough enough to run the show
He wants to know 'what the fuck is goin on'
What's Goin on?
Looks like we've confused our repertory
What's Goin On?
That's another story
That's Marvin Gaye
A few years down the way
But right now, let's see how
the worm turns
in the Kongo

Che wants to know why Kasavubu is still alive
Why Moise Tshome hasn't had his eyes nose mouth heart
plucked out
Why he's still prancin around in the south
Why the hawk of Bakongo
Why the hawk of Bakongo Bakongo
doesn't strike
Che wants to know why our enemies are still alive
He wants Lumumba to quit jivin
and start killin people
He wants his advice followed
He wants a steeper price paid
He wants Lumumba to prove that he's not afraid
to die

But, the problem is
Lumumba is more than a man
He's the living body of Mbanza Kongo
He's Africa recombined

He's the true vine
rooted once again in sacred soil
He's uncanny insight
He's the kodya shell
He's the common good
the well being of the people
You see, in Mbanza Kongo
There's no Robin Hood
There's the King
There are ritual experts who control mystic power
for the common good
But, there's no Robin Hood
There's Ndoki, the sorcerer, the individualist
the caricature, who lacks social conscience
who gets a nut then gets away
after he makes your day

Yes
Che lives in Cuba, which is Africa
But he's from Argentina, which is Italy, Germany, and Spain
It aint the same
It aint the same
It aint the same
JOHN COLTRANE!
If Lumumba just starts killing people
He kills the center
JOHN COLTRANE!
He cracks the cosmogram
He unbalances the vital world of the living
the visionary world of the dead
If he just starts killing people
perfect vision can no longer guide an imperfect world

the heart can no longer guide the head
JOHN COLTRANE!
UNDER THE GUIDE OF BROTHERLY LOVE!

Well
Nikki and Leon
The Soviet shills
Don't want Patrice Lumumba
But, they want his will
And the will of his people
Marching right in step
Into the open chasm of perpetual revolution
Which as they see it, is the final solution
To their confrontation with the West
If they can trick capital into the military industrial trade
Then their vision of the world is already made
If they can get these diamond thieves to think howitzer
instead of wire dies

To think rockets
instead of rock drills and turning tools
If they can get these warmongers to go to war forever
To be completely consumed by their creed
Which is universal greed
Which is universal greed
Which is universal greed
Then they can leave the West behind
like fallow ground never turning
Like ash, after burning
For them, the best conductors of foreign policy
are the ancient peoples of heat and electricity
Drain the West with guerrilla war

but make sure the guerrillas stay on their own shores
The Africans, the Asians, the Native peoples of sacred terrain
Who still will not accept the doctrine of total pain
Because we already live after the rain
JOHN COLTRANE!
under the guide of sexual love

J & B, John and Bobby, the American ministers of gold
get paid everyday, even when we're on hold,
they understand, that there is a plan, and you can believe
it's true
that they know every move that Nikki and Leon make
They met the chicken y'all, before it ever got baked
JOHN COLTRANE!
JOHN COLTRANE!
JOHN COLTRANE!
But deep in their hearts
they can't believe that Patrice Lumumba or Mbanza Kongo
would let go of a chance to become filthy rich
they simply can't accept
that we would reject a barbeque pit
and choose the spirit of
JOHN COLTRANE!
For J & B got to get paid
They're the ministers of gold
which is not a metal, but a standard
It measures how much better you are than the next man
How much more beautiful you are than another woman
How much more powerful you are than another human being
J & B simply can't accept that
we would reject a barbeque pit
and choose the spirit of

JOHN COLTRANE!
The American ministers of gold put everything on hold
till they get paid
You want this AIDS drug called AZT
Sucker, first you got to pay me! pay me! pay me!
You want some health insurance
You want some health insurance
You want some clothing and shelter
You need a kidney transplant
You need a skin-graft
You got heart disease
Go on and get in line
and let's see if you can pay me
For the ministers, manganese is not a magnificent trace,
coal is never defined by its fantastic name
it means to glow without flame
lead is not an ancient element
related to depth, darkness, endurance, discipline, or passivity
to the ministers, it's only a shield against radioactivity
They simply can't accept
that we would reject a barbeque pit
and choose the spirit of
JOHN COLTRANE!
JOHN COLTRANE!
JOHN COLTRANE!

ALABAMA

For
Addie Mae Collins
Denise McNair
Cynthia Wesley
Carole Robinson

Alba Ayamule
Choctaw for "I Make A Clearing"

Prelude

Monk loved
To make a clearing
And Trane
Loved Monk

The phone would ring
And it would be Trane
Laughing
Like he might be having
A relapse
Laughing so hard
Sounds like his voice
Might be tumbling backwards
Through his mouth
Through his gullet
Collapse his lung
Going south

He says,
"I need to laugh;
 fact is, I need a laugh-and-a-half"

"Man
Come on,
Let's go watch Monk
Put his clothes on"

I remember Trane
Arriving in flame
And sheets of sound

I remember Trane
Going out
In superconsciousness and serenity

I remember Trane
He made Alabama
Into a beautiful word
Again

Alabama! Alabama! Alabama!

* *

I wouldn't go there.
Martin Luther King, Jr.,
Memphis, Tennessee, April 3, 1968

You know
If I were   standing
At the beginning of time
And I had the ability
To view
The whole
Of human history
And the Most High
Lord of Creation
Asked me which age?
Which nation
Would you like to live in?
I would ask that my body
Be sent to Egypt
To become a hard poem
A block of granite
On the limestone face
Of the great pyramid
A reflector
Of the Great Sun
RA

But
In spite of his magnificence
I wouldn't stop there!
I would move on

With my flight of mind
To Meroe
Where the Queen of Sheba
Showed King Solomon
That wisdom
Sometimes is not enough
To overcome
The primal need to come
Where the word of Ethiopia
First cast her arms out over the world

But
in spite
Of her sexual offering
Her spiritual seduction
I wouldn't stop there!
I would send my soul
On to Turkey
And the age of the Seljuk
And let it bask
In the eternal whirling
Of the Mevlevi Dervishes
Seek out their services
And sit
With Jallaludin Rumi
As he composed
His ultimate love song
The Mathnawi

I would pray with him
And kneel
And wait

In the mosque
For martyrdom
For the heel
Of ignorance and suspicion
And jealousy
To strike down
The only human being
Who could heal the rift
Seal the agreement
Give the gift
Of unconditional love
Back to Rumi
Shams-ed-din
The 'Kdir'
The one who is expected
But never accepted

But:
I wouldn't stop there!
I would send my spirit on
To the Harlem renaissance
Where James P/ Johnson
And Lucky Roberts
And Willie 'The Lion'
Weaned Duke Ellington
Where Booker T.
Confronted W.E.B.
And where Marcus Garvey
First materialized
The power of the Black sea
Where Langston met Zora
For a minute

But, there was nothing in it
Where Josephine first found time
To shine
Where Black was plentiful and beautiful
And real
And surreal
Where Ho Chi Minh
Washes dishes in a soup kitchen
In Harlem
Like a hermit
Waiting for terms
That would make his own revolution
Where at five in the afternoon
Federico Garcia Lorca crooned
The Poem In New York

But,
In spite of the Black fire
Generated
From the western world's
First Black capitol
I wouldn't stop there!
I would move on
Into the twenty-sixth year
Of the twentieth century
To be exact
By the time and clock
The autumn equinox
And I would watch the birth
Of a baby
To a Kongo father
And a Yoruba mother

In a hamlet
In North Carolina

His swaddling clothes
His oppressed and marginal status
Remind us
Of another place another time
Another baby
With the same initials
J.C.

But,
In spite of the prophetic signs
And the changing times
I wouldn't stop there!

Strangely enough
I would turn to the Most High
Lord of Creation
The Living God
And say
"If you would allow me to live for six years,
in the second half of the twentieth century,
I will be satisfied. If you would allow me
To live from 1961-1967, I will be satisfied."

The ride ends February 1, 1961
It's done!
We're at the IT club, in L.A.
There's no way
We can get in to see Trane
We're children

Both seventeen
Me and Charles
That means there ain't no hope
But we stand, anyway, outside the door
Waiting for just a wisp of the horn
That has kept us alive
And whole and soulful
In the midst of this American nonsense
This pretense that there was life on earth
Before Trane
The guy at the door
About six foot four
Is eyeing us
It looks like a bust
As he moves directly toward us
Presumably to make our day
But instead of shoo-fly, don't bother me
The brother invites us in
Treats us like men
And we ain't got a dime
Miraculously
For us
It's now prime time
In L.A.

Trane and Elvin
McCoy and Jimmy
Are making the place
Shake and shimmy
But it's mostly Elvin and Trane
Both shorter than I thought
More muscular

The music stands against their flesh
Like spiritual wrought iron
The time is heat seeking
We're in a sweat

Trane's horn is hanging and singing
Humping and screaming
No more song, no more form
No more song, no more form
No more song, no more form
Four dead Black girls will be reborn
In Alabama, In Alabama, In Alabama

Suddenly Trane's lips burst
First they soak the mouthpiece
Then the blood runs down his arm
And circles his waist
Like a red sash
We're past the points of reason
And strategy and mind
We're outside of time
Inside pure energy
No more song, no more form
No more song, no more form
No more song, no more form
Four dead Black girls will be reborn
In Alabama, In Alabama, In Alabama

Trane's head is a flame
A blood red burnt crimson lake
The stakes are so high
Materially

Mentally
And spiritually
That
I turn on Charles
My own mind coming apart
And start screaming
I DON'T CARE!
I DON'T CARE!
I DON'T CARE!
I DON'T CARE!
I DON'T CARE!
I DON'T CARE!
I DON'T CARE!
I DON'T CARE!
What
They
Do
To
Me

I'll stop right there!

ELECTRIC CHURCH

I wanted to meet God
Be her spiritual ramrod
I wanted to mix and mingle
THEN RIDE LOVE UPSTREAM
Like thirty million long distance lone rangers
Ridin a black sunbeam
I wanted to deliberately
Accelerate my mind
Drop a historical depth charge
Step outside of time
I wanted to commit
Visual forgery
Make forbidden fruit return to the orchard
Like rock n roll alchemy
I wanted the light
To return to earth
I wanted to go
To Electric Church

Well now the Baptists
Said I couldn't come in
Cuz I had a hollow
Look in my eyes
The Holy Rollers
Said I wasn't their friend
That I didn't look
SANCTIFIED
The Methodists said,
"boy you look like sulfur,
but maybe we can atone yuh"

The A.M.E. said, “uh uh, boy,
you know your breath smells like ammonia”
The Mormons said
My skin was too dark
THAT NOAH HADN’T INTENDED
FOR MY BLACK ASS TO BE ON THE ARK
But I just wanted the light
To return to earth
I just wanted to go
To Electric Church

Well now the Catholics
Didn’t like me
Cuz I wouldn’t be baptized
The Jews got mad
Cuz I used to make
Pigfoot pies
The Muslims got upset
Cuz my old lady
Wore her panties on the outside
The Buddhists turned me out
Cuz I wouldn’t close down
My third eye
But I just wanted the light
To return to earth
I just wanted to go
To Electric Church

I’m wearin red cowboy boots
I’m bearin hog-head cheese,
I’m ridin a golden locust
I think God, she would be pleased

I wanted the light
To return to the earth
I wanted to go
To Electric Church

My head was hangin
Cryin fiery tears
Y'all fucked me up
For a coupla years
But now I'm back
From the universe
THE MYSTERY
Is in reverse

The damage that
Once was done
That tore me up
And made me run
Is now a note
That bends my face
And lets me void
Both time and space

I'm wearin red cowboy boots
I'm bearin hog-head cheese
I'm ridin a golden locust
I think God, she would be pleased
I brought the light
Back to the earth
I'm sittin right now
In Electric Church

TALKING IN TONGUES

I speak jackal
I speak wolf
I speak white bull

I speak bruised burro
Instead of horse or mule

I use the secret tongue
I intend
The infinite herb dialect

In the beehives of the world
I take the whole tonic of honey
Swallow it
And assume
The transformed language
Of hawk
Of heron
Of black mockingbird

I drink one cup of mescal
Twist my tongue
Into an impossible helix
With an improbable double motion

I speak crow

MEXICO

In Mexico
The blue gum
Has a human history
Because it has been ravished
By men

It has been burned by men
And then
Relegated to the territory
Of dark gruel

Once
It regenerated bladders
Cleansed kidneys
Cured tuberculosis
Calmed asthma
Cooled bronchitis

Once it talked with wild fig trees
And lived high on a plain
With light and windswept rock

Now it lives
In a small grove
And grows alone

HOLLYWOOD, 1954: THE OASIS CLUB

Bird stood alone in his dressing room wondering how his life had come to this. He and Lester Young, Bird and Prez, The two greatest Jazz saxophonists of the modern era, relegated to the dubious 'honor' of opening an obscure nite-club in Hollywood!!

The word scorched his being. Hollywood!! Like Kansas City, it was a town that had come to signify, in his mind, the lowest common denominator of the entertainment life. American Kitsch, crass commercialism, relentless exploitation of the artist and an imprint of racism deeply imbedded beneath a veneer of liberal sexual politics and a lethal drug culture.

Bird heard a soft thump-thump-thump on the dressing room door. Before he could reach out to turn the brass nob, the door swung open as if blown by a soft wind. There, silhouetted against the open door—there was suddenly something sacred in the air, as if the doorway was being transformed, or maybe relocated to some new ground that could support intense consciousness—the President, Lester Young, soaked in a gin mist so strong even Bird felt a flush of embarrassment at the paradox of a man called the President, stoned out of his mind and planted tree-like in the doorway of a dressing room in some obscure Jazz club at 2 o'clock in the afternoon. Prez, in his majesty, and in the last nine yards of a highly influential, but strange and bittersweet life, stood and sulked. Bird *moved his head* first, cocking it to the left, in feigned wonder, and then moving the incredible and malleable mask that was his face, he made ready to greet his mentor. But, Prez *spoke* first. "Lady Bird, I feel some lil two dollar whore, standin here in your door waitin for my call."

BACK TO THE LAND: CHARLIE PARKER STANDING ON LESTER YOUNG'S SHOULDERS

He called me
Back
To the land
And showed me the music
In the soil
He said
Get down Bird
On the ground
He said
Put your lips
To the earth
It's rebirth
Time

He inscribed time
He stamped harmony
He was the woodblock hipster "at the woodside"
He engraved these words
Into the crumbling red clay
Of the blues
"If a man wants to be beautiful, Bird,
He has to come back
To the Land
He has to eat loam
He has to plan
He has to build a home
In the living forest"
He said
"For us, Bird, for us,

the music is a forest
Of fantastic and principled trees
A spiritual grove
Where our Masters stand;
The branches are like the generations of man
Reaching out to us, Bird
The leaves are like the hands
Of life strategy
Biological tactic
Genetic wit
We were blown into the west, Bird
By the winds of sexual love"

He cancelled 384 shore leaves
And
Called me back to the land
And
Eclipsed himself
After thirteen adobe lifetimes

He was the ecstatic mortar
I used
To build my kingdom

He was a spark in my heart!

He called me
Back
To the land
He gave me 463 keys,
Codes
Lamps

Lights
Mystic insurance
Guarantees

He said
The circuit breaker
Would be called
Spiritual endurance

He said
Always
Always
Hold your real song in reserve

He said
Never
Never
Share
Or show
What you really know

He said
Your soul
Is s'posed to be
Your back-up

He said
Your face
Is s'posed to be
Your license
To fuckup
He said
To find True Freedom
You gotta do something expected today

But you gotta do it
In an unexpected way

You gotta find a loaf
Of white bread
Then eat the black crust

I repeat
You gotta find a loaf
Of white bread
Then eat the black crust

I repeat
You gotta find a loaf
Of white bread
Then eat the black crust

Trust me Bird!

He said
"Lady Bird,"
You know
In that way he could say something
That'd circle all around you
Make your head spin
Your eyes rotate
And then break you down
Right before
He'd penetrate you
He said, "Lady Bird. Fame, say!
Money, say! women!!!"
He'd say *women* with a little New Orleans wisp

In between the whiskey scratches on his voice
"It don't mean nothin, Lady Bird,
Less you can maintain and point yo'sef
Out into the world
And know
Which way
To go
Now, Lady Bird
That ain't no bullshit.
That's *real shit!*"

I came back to the land
But
I couldn't remember the man
who'd called me

I lost the keys
I forgot the codes
I blew out the lights
Doused the lamps
I sought strange new modes
Amps
Watts
Impulse
Fluid
Magnetism
Charges of electricity
Became the city
Laid out before my eyes
My whole saxophone being
Was focused
On the thighs

Cuz, it lies between the thighs
Every day was a holiday
And
The land
Was a woman
Who moved
For me
Every day
I wrote poetry
I made sculpture
I rode herd on love
I was the man who loved women
Who ate box lunches at the Y
I took St. John to the bridge
And showed him the sperm pool of Revelation
Where the legend over the entrance
To the Jazz railway station read:
"He who loveth not, knoweth not God;
for God is love"
Inspiration became my affliction
I was a selfish gene
I set the world record for fertility
I grew golden sardines in my laboratory
When the final curtain fell
I was trying to plant a peach tree in hell

It's late in the day of March 12, 1955
I suddenly take a nosedive
And go down past grieving
I'm in the absolute evening of my life
Abandoning my mother, my friends,
My children and my wife

I choose selfishly
To assassinate myself in time
In the name of evolution
Erotic ascension
Stable biological strategy
Direct action
And spiritual economy

I lost the keys
I forgot the codes
I blew out the lights
I doused the lamps
I forfeited the guarantees
Cancelled my meetings with endurance
And cashed in my insurance

My spiritual insight was always suspect
In my life I never held one song in reserve

What I know
Finally
Is what you know

But
I came back
To the land

SILVER BULLET

One night he improvised for twenty minutes
on the Lone Ranger's theme.

> from *Bird Lives: The High Life and Hard Time of Charlie (Yardbird) Parker* by Ross Russell

Check this out:
The Lone Ranger
A stranger if ever there was one
Rides up on Silver
And declares the Be-Bop combination
The Revolution
The black crap game
Over
He insists that Jazz desist
Cease to exist

But he doesn't understand
That
To a Black man
The music is more than archaic minstrelsy
More than bittersweet symphony
The music is food
And gathered together we agree to be nourished in its name
And by its players
Bird, Babs, Miles, Max and Trane

The stranger proceeds to impede the game
Which is the music
By refusing to admit

That the music is real
That it's the last fair deal goin down

"I'm not submittin to the new cipher,
The blue symbol. The Black numeral;
Because it doesn't make sense to me,"
Says the Ranger

"My job is to keep the plains clear. You know, like
John Wayne. The Duke. I gotta make my home where
The buffalo used to roam. I gotta keep these goddam
In'juns in their place"

Tonto flinches
Furls his brow
The cinches on his palomino tighten
Now, you know, he'd like to kick the Lone Ranger's ass
But, what can he do?
The stranger is his Keemosaabey
His sho'nuff saddle-up vined-on-a-dime mask wearin

Silver-bullet-bitin homeboy
I mean
What can he do?

Max Speaks:
Look here stranger
See these drumsticks
They're like numbers, ya dig?
Ya got cardinal, whole, round, perfect, prime, serial and digit
But to get with it
Ya gotta listen

Open-up, stuff!

But the Ranger's waitin for Dixieland to return
He's lookin for Benny Goodman
To burn Fletcher Henderson's rearrangements
He's lookin for Benny to be mispronounced the King of Swing

Tonto
Obviously unnerved
By the turn of the conversation
Fidgets in his saddle
Looks for somethin to do with his hands
Nobody knows yet
That he's hanging by a thread

Babs Speaks:
I'm tryin to relate the current state of affairs to you, Ranger
Dig!
If you can sum-up the summation
Differentiate the product
Then you can re-count the reduction and induct the score
Reckon the tally, resurrect the tale, box the total
From here, you permutate the combination
Thereby, alterin the election
Ya dig??!

The stranger's perception has abandoned deception
But, he'll drop dead right here
Before he'll accept the new map of the universe
That these Black adepts have laid out
For his dinner
Like the last of the perverse

Before he'll accept reality from a Black man
He'll die first

Tonto, meanwhile, frowns on the surface
But, deep in his being, a little Tonto smiles
And says
So be it!

Trane Speaks:
In cadenced speech
Focused and dignified
Like old folks
Who never had nothin to hide

Variation says Trane
Variation is the basis of function
Ranger, if you won't change
Totally
Spiritually
If you won't agree to have your face
Ripped-off the front of your face
Then there's no hope for you

The Ranger is caught between acceptance and fear
Between what he wants and what he needs
Between the trick of his mind
And the truth of his ear
Tonto goes backward three steps
Twenty four years
Twelve generations
The akashic nations in his blood
Begin to hum a little tune

Miles Speaks:
The monster is the maker of the mischief
So What!
It's time for him to pay his dues
So what!
The time has come for us to end the bullshit
So what!
Fulfill the promise of the blues

The stranger suddenly feels old, odd, out of place
Unwelcome, ugly, vulnerable, trapped, undressed, oppressed,
Infantile, abused by the news
That human beings don't own a goddam thing on earth

Tonto
Suddenly at ease
Adjusts his gunbelt
He's just felt something warm rising in his body

It runs from the depth of his asshole
Straight-up his back
To the base of his head
Turns inward at 45 degrees
Hits the core of his brain
Smoking, focused and runnin

Somebody's comin!
Somebody's comin!
Somebody's comin!

Bird Speaks:
Ranger

All these antics you see
All this music
Is just higher mathematics
It's the final counting
Which is the telling
Which is the real computation
The casting
The harmonic bottom of dead reckoning

It's the air strike
Not against Iraq or Libya or Cuba or Grenada or Panama
Or any other small, ancient, and defenseless people

This is the final baritone abundance
That rips up the foundation of disease
That breaks the knees of racism, fascism, and capitalism
With big black basball bats

That statement is made
That account is closed
We've called the roll
We're set to sail
Ranger let's hope your check is in the mail

With nothing left to say
All the Lone Ranger's facade falls away
Not only is his mission a fraud
Not only is he finally exposed as a complete fake
But, check it out
His horse is a bay
THAT HE HAD SPRAY PAINTED WHITE!!!

He never was a Texas Ranger
He was a security guard in a grammar school
In Pocatello, Idaho
When Tonto found him dehydrated and near death
in the desert
He'd been whipped by a roving band of boy scouts
And left, not for dead
But, behind
They thought he'd be found
Because he was really on the campground
Of a state park

Check it out:
His marked pedigreed silver pistols?
They're pewter
His joy and his pride, his leather saddle?
It's naugahyde
His mask?
An attempt to hide some fucked-up plastic surgery
He wandered up and down the country
From town to western town
Out of boredom
Not urgency
He was all dressed-up
But he had no place to go

Tonto
Ready to blow
The top of his head or his horn
It makes no difference when you're gettin reborn

Infuriated by the revelations

Devastated by the music
Egged on by
Willie Best, Charlie Chan, Mantan Moreland, the Buffalo Soldiers, Tenspeed Beal, Buddy Bolden, Amos, Andy, Kingfish, Sapphire,Mustang Sally, Dr. Feelgood, Willie Horton, Mike Tyson
And the Boyz From The Hood

Tonto blows!!!

He snatches the Ranger down off of Silver
(Who, by the way, was really named Jamie;
I mean, if I was a horse you couldn't pay me
to be called Jamie anyway)
As Tonto was callin up the spirit of Cochise, Geronimo, Sittin Bull, Red Cloud, and, of course, Crazy Horse
A serious scuffle ensued
Some rude things were said
Some left hooks and right crosses
Were landed upside the Ranger's head
And some stiff native moccasins
Soaked in the endless humiliations of the past
Were seen flyin off into the Lone Ranger's ass
But, in order to make a long story short
The most important thing to note
Is that the Lone Ranger
With one short muffled shot to the throat
Met his maker
And gave up the ghost

Bird, Babs, Max, Miles and Trane
Stood

Amazed for a minute
They didn't know whether to shake Tonto's hand
Or get him out of the country
On the next airplane

Finally Bird
Quicksilver smile in place
Welcomed Tonto to the band
With the Jazz embrace

HI HO SILVER AND AWAY!!!!!!!!!!!!!

BIO

K. Curtis Lyle was born and raised in Los Angeles, California. He was a founding member of the Watts Writers Workshop, joining it in 1966 and becoming a prominent member of the Los Angeles renaissance the group represented. He has taught, lectured, and read his poetry in performance in the major intellectual and urban centers of North America. He has been Writer-in-Residence and Assistant Professor of American Literature at Washington University in St. Louis (1969-1973); Assistant Professor of English at The City College of The City University of New York (1980-1982); Specialist in Translating Experience into Essay, Curriculum Development Committee, The Faculty of The College of New Rochelle (1981-1984). He has been mentor and master teacher for the National Foundation for Advancement in the Arts in Miami, Florida and from 1988, has been Professor of Creative Writing and Cross Culture at Lindenwood College in St. Charles, Missouri. Lyle has published widely over the years and been anthologized in the United States, Canada, South America, and Europe. Several of his works, including *15 Predestination Weather Reports* (Beyond Baroque), *The Collected Poems for Blind Lemon Jefferson*, and *Drunk on God* have become underground classics. Lyle's work has been widely adapted to music, especially for jazz. He built a performing and recording relationship with the late world-renowned saxophonist and composer Julius Hemphill (1938-1995). The text of Lyle's poem, *Drunk on God*, was recorded for Julius Hemphill's Big Band (Electra/Asylum).

Lyle is committed to restoring poetry to the forefront

of performing and ritual arts, with call and response, back-up voices, the echoing of words and phrases, musical and vocal dialogues and harmonies, and choral effects of all kinds forming the high human expressive voice and speaking from a fundamental grounding in unity and ecstatic religious experience, there, seeking community and communion.

The poems in this book were selected from the following books and chapbooks: *Sometimes I Go To Camarillo and Sit in the Lounge* (1967); *Fifteen Predestination Weather Reports* (1975); *Drunk on God* (1975) and *From Out of Nowhere* (1975); *Washerwoman* (1983); *The Mystic Marriage* (1985); *Alabama* (1992); *Electric Church* (1992); *Sippin from the Holy Grail in Downtown Atlantis* (1992); *Atlantis* (1992); *Self-Defense* (1994); *The Word from Johannesberg* (1994); *Migrations* (1994); and *Curandera* (1997).

from the warring factions, Ammiel Alcalay $12
Princess Freak, Nancy Agabian $10
American Zen Bones: Maezumi Roshi Stories, Philomene Long $10
Muddy Shoes, Majid Naficy $8
Black Love, Michael Datcher, ed. $8
Echo 681, Wednesday Night Poetry Workshop $8
Paper Frankenstein, Eve Wood $5
This Just In, Joel Brouwer $5
A Voice In The Garden, Sandor Tádjèck/Kurt Brown $5

OTHER PUBLICATIONS

Harbinger: Fiction and Poetry by Los Angeles Writers,
Terry Wolverton & Benjamin Weissman, eds.
(co-published with the L.A. Festival) $8
FOREHEAD Writing & Art Journal, Vol's 1 & 2,
Benjamin Weissman, Paul Vangelisti, Amy Gerstler,
Don Suggs, Lane Relyea, eds. $7
Chinese Folk Poetry, translated by Cecilia Liang $4

For orders & distribution,
please call SPD at (800) 869-7553